Legion o

Honor | Inside and Out

Introduction by Ann Heath Karlstrom

New photography by Henrik Kam

Published by the Fine Arts Museums of San Francisco

SPACES | Collections

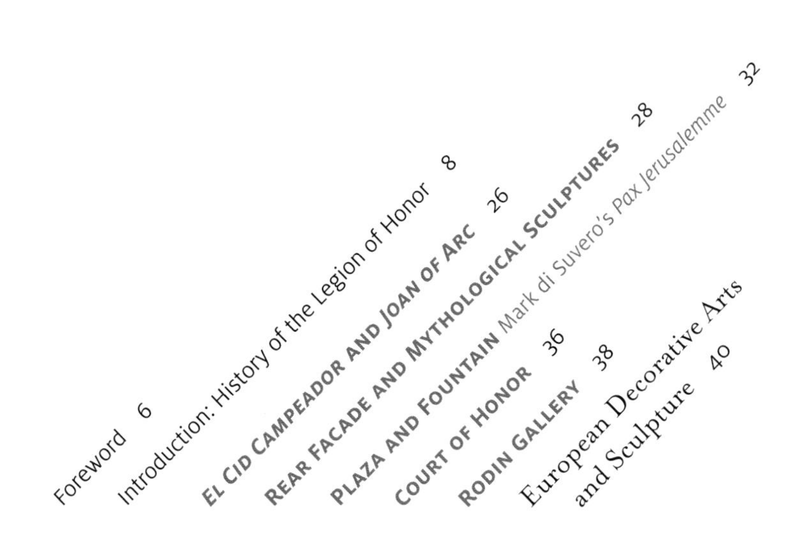

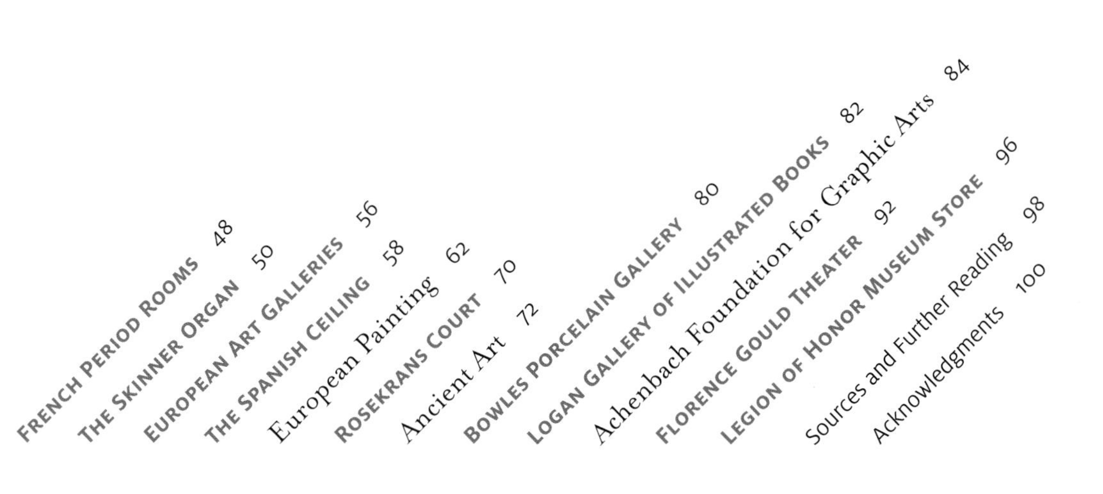

CHOIR
UNISON
OFF
NAZARD
FLUTE
CELESTE
8

FOREWORD

THE LEGION OF HONOR is my favorite museum in San Francisco. Not only is it a site of unequalled beauty, filled with great art, but it also holds an important place in San Francisco and US history. Conceived by Alma de Bretteville Spreckels, the Legion was built as a memorial to California soldiers killed in World War I and sits at the very terminus of the Lincoln Highway, the first road to cross America.

High on a promontory overlooking sweeping views of the Golden Gate, the Beaux-Arts building contains six millennia of ancient and European art. Greeting visitors in the beautiful Court of Honor is the brooding and imposing bronze cast of Rodin's *The Thinker*, a statue purchased by Alma herself. Generations of San Franciscans have gathered at the Legion to view exhibitions, listen to music, enjoy a meal, or just look at the views.

The Legion combines with the de Young to form the Fine Arts Museums of San Francisco, holding one of the largest memberships of any art museum in the United States. We are very proud of the ongoing support of our members and patrons, which attests to the importance they place on our mission to provide excellent art exhibitions, educational programs, and conservation of the art entrusted to us.

More than one hundred years after their beginnings, the Fine Arts Museums continue to serve as one of the premier public arts institutions in the world. I am sure you will find the Legion as inspiring and beautiful as I do.

Diane B. Wilsey
President, Board of Trustees

One of a pair of lions in front of the Legion of Honor in the fog, with the statue of Joan of Arc in the background.

INTRODUCTION: HISTORY OF THE LEGION OF HONOR

PRESIDING OVER one of San Francisco's most beautiful views, the California Palace of the Legion of Honor boasts a stunning physical presence and a history that is almost equally dramatic. The French neoclassical building looks out onto the Pacific Ocean as it flows through the Golden Gate and into the bay in a grand convergence of city, land, sea, and sky (see pages 24–25). The building and the institution it houses were created for the citizens of San Francisco by Alma de Bretteville Spreckels, whose modest origins belie the power and influence she summoned in making this cultural gift to the city.

Alma de Bretteville (fig. 1, left) was born in 1881 to a poor family on a farm in what is now the Sunset District of San Francisco. In her mid-teens she quit school to help support her family and was soon working as a stenographer. She also attended evening classes at the Mark Hopkins Institute of Art. A beautiful young woman—and unusually tall, at six feet—Alma found that she could work as an artist's model to help pay for her classes. The sculptor Robert Aitken, who taught at the institute, asked her to pose for the figure of Victory that tops the Dewey Monument in Union Square. The unveiling of the statue in 1903 added to the attention that Alma was already attracting in San Francisco as a venturesome and ambitious individual. This included the notice of Adolph B. Spreckels, (fig. 1, right) a member of the wealthy family that owned, among other enterprises, the Spreckels sugar refineries. Alma set out to become his wife, but it took some time. The earthquake of 1906, which devastated the city, left the figure of Victory standing, and its model proved equally stalwart. Though she reportedly turned her energies to the relief efforts in the tent city that sprang up in Golden Gate Park while Adolph dealt with the

Inside the Legion, Auguste Rodin's *The Age of Bronze* stands in the center of the Rotunda.

Fig. 1
Alma de Bretteville (shown in 1906) and Adolph B. Spreckels (in an undated photograph) would become the founders of the California Palace of the Legion of Honor.

damage to his parents' home and the family businesses, by 1908 Alma had refocused and convinced Adolph to marry her. The uninhibited Mrs. Spreckels then began her campaign to conquer San Francisco society.

With the Spreckels wealth, Alma embarked on a new and extravagant life. The newlyweds honeymooned in Europe, giving Alma her first experience of French culture. Not long after their return to San Francisco she convinced her husband to let her build a French château in Pacific Heights. It was completed in 1913, after three years of construction. Nothing like it had been built in the city since the great railroad barons' mansions of the 1870s. Alma wanted to fill her château with eighteenth-century furnishings, which conveyed status and elegance appropriate to the new station in life she was creating for herself. These could not be found locally, so Adolph encouraged her to travel to France.

In 1914 Alma set out for Paris alone and with no knowledge of the French language, but aided by Adolph's money and introductions to fine art dealers. Among the luminaries she met was the flamboyant American modern dancer Loïe Fuller, famous for her colorful performances in which she swirled yards of brilliant silk attached to long wands. The two women soon became friends, Loïe having spent enough time in Paris to serve as Alma's guide in purchasing antiques and

Fig. 2
The Palais de la Légion d'Honneur in Paris, seen here in a lithograph by J. Devicque, dated 1861, was the architectural model for the new museum in San Francisco.

furnishings. Recognizing an avid art collector in the making, Loïe introduced the rich and enthusiastic visitor to the work of Auguste Rodin. Having appointed herself as his agent, she was determined that Alma meet the artist. Showing "the Master" a photograph of Alma's new home at 2080 Washington Street, Loïe called it a "museum." Alma did not correct the misrepresentation, as her intentions were already pointed in that direction. Bringing back furniture and tapestries, as well as other antiques, Alma soon set up a gallery in her house. Through her friendship with Loïe, she also took the first steps toward acquiring works by Rodin.

By the time Alma returned, World War I was beginning in Europe. Nevertheless, France was eventually convinced to go forward with its plans to participate in the Panama Pacific International Exposition of 1915 and sent objects for the exhibition on a US Navy coal ship. Loïe made sure that Rodin sculptures were included, with Alma paying for their freight. The French pavilion at the exposition, modeled after the Palais de la Légion d'Honneur in Paris, was constructed by architect Henri Guillaume in a mere three months. There Rodin's sculptures were prominently displayed, with *The Thinker* placed in the center of its front courtyard. When the Spreckelses visited the pavilion, Alma immediately decided that it was the perfect setting for Rodin's work. She had already begun making arrangements to purchase many of these sculptures, and because the pavilion was built as a temporary structure, Alma persuaded her husband that the museum they had been considering should become a permanent re-creation of the building.

Alma was undaunted by the existence of the Memorial Museum (later renamed the M. H. de Young Memorial Museum, to honor its founder) in Golden Gate Park; it was at that time not strictly an art museum and certainly not focused on the arts of France. Neither she nor Adolph apparently gave any thought to the fact that in 1884, when he was twenty-seven years old, Adolph had shot and wounded "Mike" de Young after de Young's *San Francisco Chronicle* newspaper had accused the Spreckels Sugar Company of criminal labor practices. (De Young survived, and Spreckels was acquitted after a plea of "impulsive insanity.") So Alma embarked upon her project, which would take almost a decade to realize.

Alma and Adolph had already selected architect George Applegarth to build a museum in a spot donated by the Park Commissioners: two square blocks in Alta

Fig. 3
Alma de Bretteville Spreckels lays the cornerstone for the new museum.

Fig. 4
Construction of the Legion of Honor began in the remote Lands End site in the northwest corner of San Francisco.

Plaza Park between Scott and Pierce Streets, below Jackson. Applegarth had designed their home at 2080 Washington Street and was well respected in the city. After the exposition, however, Alma found the designated site inadequate. There are several versions of the story of how she selected a new setting for the museum. In one, Loïe Fuller pointed to the spot in a characteristically dramatic gesture while the two women were conducting their search for a location at Lands End. The greatest likelihood, however, is that Applegarth helped choose the site. A related tale claims that the chosen location was so close to the putting greens for the seventeenth hole of a public golf course that Alma announced she would ask the golf course architect, W. Herbert Fowler, to redesign the hole in order to placate the golfers. In any case, the golf course remains, and Lands End became the spectacular setting for Alma's French museum.

The Parisian model for the French pavilion that inspired Alma's new plans was first called the Hôtel de Salm, and had also influenced Thomas Jefferson's architecture at Monticello. It was designed by Pierre Rousseau and built between 1782 and 1787 for the German Prince Frederick III of Salm-Kyrburg. The prince lived there for only a year before his fortunes were altered by the French Revolution; he was guillotined in 1794. After the Revolution, the author and political figure Madame de Staël took over the building and held many of her literary salons there. But her political currency also ran out, and in 1804 the palace was nationalized to house the Légion d'Honneur, an order created by Napoléon Bonaparte to recognize civil and military merit. Political upheaval again intervened and the Palais de la Légion d'Honneur was destroyed by the fire of 1871, during the Paris Commune. It was soon rebuilt and stands in Paris to this day (fig. 2).

At the close of the Panama-Pacific Exposition, the French government agreed to the Spreckelses' request to construct a permanent replica of the Palais de la Légion d'Honneur in San Francisco, but World War I delayed its progress. Finally, in December 1921, Marshal Foch of France came for the groundbreaking ceremony, planting a Monterey cypress near the remote but spectacular site at Lands End. Applegarth provided the design for a three-quarter-scale version of the exterior of the original building and oversaw its construction. To the interior he brought the most advanced ideas for climate control of the time:

HONNEUR ET PATRIE
RF

twenty-one-inch-thick walls of hollow tiles to stabilize temperatures, and a heating system without radiators that filtered air through atomizers to eliminate dust.

The building was completed in 1924, but Alma presided over its opening alone; Adolph had died four months earlier. The Legion, dedicated "to honor the dead while serving the living," opened to the public on Armistice Day, November 11, 1924 (fig. 5), and was accepted by the city as a museum and memorial to the 3,600 California men who had died on the battlefields of France. As part of the opening ceremony, after honoring the late Adolph as a founder of the museum, a representative from the French government awarded Alma the Cross of the Legion of Honor—a fitting culmination of her campaign and recognition of her efforts both to bring aid to France during the war and to bring French art to her country.

By the time her museum opened, Alma had acquired the first of the more than eighty Rodin sculptures in plaster, terracotta, marble, and bronze that she would donate to the Legion over nearly thirty-five years (figs. 6, 7). The French Republic made gifts of tapestries, Sèvres vases, medals, and coins, while other French supporters joined forces to provide more works of art, and even furnished

Fig. 5
The California Palace of the Legion of Honor opened on November 11, 1924.

rooms, for the museum. Alma's connections and friendships with Loïe Fuller and others in French artistic circles helped her build a distinguished collection of drawings and sculptures, as well as costumes and set designs related to dance and opera.

Though her focus centered primarily on French and other European arts, Alma also promoted the work of American sculptor Arthur Putnam, who had met Rodin in Paris and whose sculptures reflected his influence. She had previously taken plasters of Putnam's work to France to be cast by Rodin's *fondeur*, Rudier, so that they could be displayed at the Panama-Pacific International Exposition, where they were awarded a gold medal. In her new museum Alma displayed a substantial number of Putnam's sculptures in a gallery of their own. She had earlier reported that he was the only California artist who had offered to give artworks to her museum. The collection of European art, meanwhile, continued to grow rapidly through gifts from friends and museum patrons. Alma was never afraid to ask for what she thought would benefit the Legion, and the responses she received set the stage for generous donations that continued well beyond the years of her leadership.

As time went on, unexpected riches came to the museum. The Achenbach Foundation for Graphic Arts, established by Mr. and Mrs. Moore S. Achenbach and given to the city of San Francisco in 1948, was moved from the public library to the Legion of Honor in 1950. Enhanced by many gifts that followed, including the Reva and David Logan Collection of Illustrated Books, given

Fig. 6
On the museum's opening day, Auguste Rodin's *The Thinker* already commanded a place of prominence in the Court of Honor, where it remains today (see pages 36–37).

Fig. 7
A gallery in the museum is filled with additional works by Rodin in an undated photo from the mid-twentieth century.

in 2000, the Fine Arts Museums of San Francisco's Achenbach Foundation is home to the largest collection of works on paper in the western United States.

The administration of Alma's gift to the city began awkwardly. In 1923, prior to the opening of the museum, the president of the Park Commission, Herbert Fleishhacker, appointed Arthur Upham Pope to be the director. He was a noted historian of Persian art—not at all what Alma had in mind. By 1924 she installed her own choice: Cornelia Bentley Sage Quinton, formerly the director of the Albright-Knox Art Gallery in Buffalo, New York, whom she had met in 1914 at the same dinner party where she had met Loïe Fuller. Quinton was followed in 1931 by Lloyd LaPage Rollins, who was also director of the de Young until 1933. Walter Heil then assumed the position of director of both museums until 1939, when he was succeeded by Thomas Carr Howe Jr., who had been an assistant director at the Legion of Honor. Meanwhile, as the years passed and her health diminished, Alma withdrew from active participation in museum matters. Howe was assisted in the last years of his tenure by Ian McKibbin White, who became director upon Howe's retirement in 1968.

Fig. 8
Sir John Lavery (English, 1856–1941). *Alma de Bretteville Spreckels (Mrs. Adolph B. Spreckels)*, 1932. Oil on canvas, 46 x 36 in. (116.8 x 91.4 cm). Gift of Alma de Bretteville Spreckels, 1951.40

Alma's death, also in 1968, marked the end of an era. In 1970 the boards of the Legion of Honor and the de Young decided their common purposes would be more successfully realized if they became one institution. The two museums, formed by families that had been archrivals on issues other than art collecting, were united as one cultural gift to the city. After a trial period of two years the Fine Arts Museums of San Francisco became a new single entity, with White as director.

In 1972 Alma's grandson Adolph Rosekrans and his architectural firm, Rosekrans and Broder, completed a redesign of the Legion's main sculpture gallery, for which White himself had designed the pedestals. The project was funded by the Patrons of Art and Music, a support organization established by Alma in 1956. The purpose of the redesign was to better display the entire collection of Rodin sculptures. Over the entrance to the gallery, the Spreckels name appeared on the building for the first time: "Adolph B. and Alma de Bretteville Spreckels Sculpture Gallery." The Hélène Irwin Fagan bequest in 1975 brought not only art but also additional funds to support Rosekrans and Broder's expansion of the building's galleries and office spaces.

In 1979 another event presented the opportunity to make beneficial changes to the building. The enormous exhibition *The Splendor of Dresden* entailed no less than a complete deinstallation of the permanent holdings at the Legion. The museum was temporarily reconfigured for that display, and new climate control was added. At the close of *Dresden* the permanent collections were presented in refurbished galleries as a special exhibition, *The Heritage of France.* This exhibition emphasized the reorganization of the collections of the two museums under White's direction, with the Legion of Honor featuring the arts of France.

Other changes also improved the museum's interior; the Rosekrans firm supervised the renovation of the Little Theater (now the Florence Gould Theater), and French restorers brought its ceiling mural to new magnificence in 1987 (see pages 92–95). But by this time it was increasingly evident that the Legion of Honor needed to be made more seismically secure—in spite of the seven thousand cubic yards of concrete and the one million pounds of reinforcing bars in the original structure. When Ian White retired in 1987 Harry S. Parker III became director, and that need was soon underlined. The damage caused by the Loma Prieta earthquake of 1989 left no choice but to act, so between 1992 and 1995 the Legion underwent a substantial renovation by the architects Edward Larrabee Barnes and Mark Cavagnero. Fittingly, the museum reopened on Armistice Day, November 11, 1995, the building's seventy-first anniversary. The collections had again been rearranged, with all antiquities and European works of art displayed in the Legion as part of Parker's vision for the strongest presentation of the holdings of the combined museums.

After renovations, the historic facade of the refurbished building remains the same, though Rodin's *The Thinker* now shares the courtyard with a glass pyramid that offers adjustable natural light to an interior court below. In addition to seismic upgrades, improved building systems, and restored architectural features, the museum gained 35,000 square feet in an underground expansion. Six new galleries for special exhibitions surround the lower court, and the nationally recognized paper conservation laboratory doubled in size to better serve as a training center. A new print study room provides not only computerized workstations for access to the collection, but also the space and opportunity for supervised close examinations of works on paper. Across the hall, the Porcelain Study Room, adjacent to the porcelain gallery, allows scholars to study examples from that part of the museum's collection as well.

Of course, improvement of services for general visitors was also a goal of the renovation. An expansive new café opens onto a patio, offering a relaxing dining experience and striking views of both the garden areas and the Pacific Ocean. Opposite the restaurant, the enlarged museum store features items that relate to the collections and special exhibitions.

The original construction of the California Palace of the Legion of Honor was paid for entirely by Adolph B. Spreckels—at more than one million dollars in 1924, it cost, like most such projects, more than had been expected. By the time of her death, Alma's fortunes had been much reduced—by both her generosity and her lifestyle. Support for the renovation of the building completed in 1995 had to come through a different and

Fig. 9
The Legion's renovation, seen here in 1994, included an underground expansion.

HONNEUR ET PATRIE

much more complicated process that combined public and private funds. San Francisco voters approved public bonds for the seismic upgrade, asbestos removal, and improved accessibility for visitors with disabilities. The National Endowment for the Arts awarded a challenge grant for the project, and the balance of funding came primarily from private donations. Mr. and Mrs. John N. Rosekrans Jr. chaired the campaign to raise those funds, extending in some measure the Spreckels legacy: John Rosekrans was the oldest grandson of Adolph and Alma Spreckels. His wife, Dodie Rosekrans, also chaired the board of trustees through the completion of the renovation.

The expanded and improved Legion of Honor thrived under the direction of Parker, who retired in 2005, and his successor, John E. Buchanan, Jr., who was director from 2006 until his untimely death in late 2011. Today the collections begun by Alma Spreckels continue to grow, and a vigorous exhibition program perpetuates the drama and excitement that she envisioned for her museum overlooking the Pacific.

Fig. 10
An aerial photograph of the Legion of Honor shows its spectacular setting at the edge of the Golden Gate.

EL CID CAMPEADOR AND *JOAN OF ARC*

Two monumental bronze equestrian sculptures, *El Cid Campeador* and *Joan of Arc*, stand on the lawn on either side of the Legion of Honor. Both are the work of Anna Hyatt Huntington, one of this country's most eminent sculptors of the twentieth century.

Joan of Arc, the Maid of Orléans, led the French army to several important victories in the Hundred Years' War. The first casting of *Joan of Arc*, completed by the artist (then Anna Vaughn Hyatt) in 1915, was unveiled on Riverside Drive in New York City. It won her the purple rosette of the government of France and later the insignia of Chevalier de la Légion d'Honneur. In 1923 Hyatt married Archer M. Huntington, founder of the Hispanic Society of America and son of Arabella Huntington (wife of Henry E. Huntington, who founded the Huntington Library). Three years later he presented the Legion of Honor with this full-size replica, one of four that were cast from the original. The other casts are in Blois, France; in Gloucester, Massachusetts; and on the Plains of Abraham historic battlefield park, in Québec City, Québec.

Archer Huntington was not only a patron of the arts but also a scholar. His translation of the Spanish epic *Poema de Mio Cid* inspired Anna Hyatt Huntington to model this figure of the eleventh-century hero Rodrigo Díaz de Vivar, who became known as El Cid Campeador. El Cid was a military champion of King Alfonso VI of Léon and Castile, and he gained the title of Campeador (champion or challenger) through his important victories against the forces of Granada. The original statue, cast in 1927, is in Seville, Spain. This cast, presented to the museum in 1937 by Herbert Fleishhacker, is also one of four full-size replicas. The others are in Buenos Aires; at the Hispanic Society of America in New York City; and in Balboa Park, San Diego.

REAR FACADE AND MYTHOLOGICAL SCULPTURES

Around the cupola on the rear facade of the Legion of Honor stand six statues of classical mythological figures: Jupiter, Mars, Apollo, Minerva, Diana, and Ceres. They were modeled on the sculptures added to the Palais de la Légion d'Honneur in Paris when it was nationalized by Napoléon in 1804. Those works, by Jean Guillaume Moitte and Philippe-Laurent Roland, were destroyed by the Commune fires in 1871 and replaced by copies that are now in the Musée de la Légion d'Honneur.

The nine-foot-tall, three-thousand-pound statues placed on this building in 1924 suffered decades of exposure to salt air and ocean winds and eventually began to disintegrate; by the 1980s pieces of concrete were dropping to the ground. The sculptures, supported by rusting one-inch steel bars, were removed at great effort and taken to the San Francisco studio of sculptor and restorer Manuel Palos. He made repairs and rubber molds to recast them after going to Paris to study the copies there. His new reproductions, installed in 1989, are composed of fiberglass resin and pulverized limestone. Much lighter and more durable than their predecessors, they are anchored through interior metal reinforcement. Once the new reproductions were complete, the damaged ones were destroyed.

The thirteen busts in the round niches lining the building below are also modeled on the original French architecture. Better protected from the elements, they have survived without restoration.

A Laocoön figure grouping (detail right) is also located at the rear of the building, visible through the lower-level glass doors.

PLAZA AND FOUNTAIN
MARK DI SUVERO'S
PAX JERUSALEMME

AT THE CENTER of the round pool in front of the Legion of Honor, a splashing fountain animates this tranquil section of the city, otherwise brought to life by golfers and occasional wildlife. On the rare still and sunny days, if the fountain is quiet, visitors can enjoy a clear reflection of the museum's colonnaded facade.

Few may know that this is the western terminus of the Lincoln Highway, the first transcontinental road for automobiles. The highway originally began at Times Square in New York City and ran almost 3,400 miles, across thirteen states, to this endpoint. Dedicated on October 31, 1913, it was the first national memorial to President Abraham Lincoln, predating the completion of the Lincoln Memorial in Washington, DC, by nine years. A plaque at the southwest corner of the plaza marks the end of the highway.

Beyond the pool stands the bright red abstract sculpture *Pax Jerusalemme,* by Mark di Suvero. Completed and installed in 1999, it was chosen as a modern, symmetrical response to the more classical museum building—an exclamation point to energize the space.

ALEXANDER AND JEAN DE BRETTEVILLE COURT OF HONOR

AUGUSTE RODIN'S *The Thinker* has presided over the Court of Honor, leading to the entrance to the Legion of Honor, since the museum's opening in 1924. Acquired in 1915 by museum founder Alma de Bretteville Spreckels, the sculpture announces the importance of Rodin's work to the beginnings of the Legion, as well as this collection's continued standing as among the world's most comprehensive. The Alexander and Jean de Bretteville Court of Honor is named for one of Alma's brothers and his second wife. Alexander stood by Alma and acted as her business manager throughout her life.

With the museum's renovation in 1995 a glass pyramid was added in the court, providing a contrast to the stone pavers that fill the space. An echo of the pyramid designed by I. M. Pei and completed in 1989 for the courtyard at the Musée du Louvre in Paris, this addition brings natural light to Rosekrans Court and the surrounding galleries on the lower level of the museum, which were expanded with the renovation.

RODIN GALLERY

The first work of art to greet visitors at the Legion of Honor is Auguste Rodin's *The Thinker* (page 47), given to the museum for its opening in 1924. Within the museum, Rodin's *The Age of Bronze* stands in the Rotunda (see page 8). Further inside is a room identified as the Adolph B. and Alma de Bretteville Spreckels Gallery. Although sculptures may rotate in and out of view, the space is usually dominated by Rodin's *The Three Shades*, flanked by his *Saint John the Baptist Preaching* and *The Prodigal Son*. Other pieces by Rodin stand along the walls, and galleries on either side offer a rare opportunity to see his bronze works and unique plasters displayed together.

Over the passageway leading back to the entry is a set of bronze letters announcing the "Adolph B. and Alma de Bretteville Spreckels Rodin Gallery Dedicated 11 November 1974, the 50th Anniversary of This Museum, Their Gift to San Francisco." Alma Spreckels first purchased works by Rodin in 1915, acquiring many casts made during the artist's lifetime. The placement of these works in the introductory galleries of the museum is an appropriate recognition of the Legion's distinction as the home of one of the three most important collections of Rodin sculptures outside the Musée Rodin in Paris.

European Decorative Arts and Sculpture

THE DEPARTMENT OF European decorative arts and sculpture encompasses a diverse array of works from across the continent, dating from the Middle Ages to the early twentieth century. Its holdings were crucial to the original vision for the Legion of Honor and remain emblematic of the museum today.

Inspired by her distant French noble ancestry and sympathy for France in World War I, founder Alma de Bretteville Spreckels wanted the Legion to reflect a specifically French identity in both its architecture and its founding collection. To this end she formed one of the most important holdings of Auguste Rodin's work outside France, a group of some eighty-one sculptures made during the artist's lifetime that has become a centerpiece of the entire museum and includes what is now its signature image, *The Thinker* (page 47). Spreckels's many other significant contributions to the collection include sculptures by Rodin's contemporary Théodore Rivière, French Empire silver, and European porcelain. She also worked fervently to cultivate donations such as the remarkable Fabergé tea table and tea service presented by Victoria Melita, Grand Duchess Kirill of Russia (left); wonderful examples of French eighteenth-century furniture, mounted porcelain, and sculpture from Archer M. Huntington; the Mildred Anna Williams collection of French eighteenth-century decorative arts, given by Henry K. S. Williams; and a selection of contemporary and historic Sèvres porcelain donated by the French government.

The Legion's collection of European decorative arts and sculpture has evolved significantly since Spreckels's time. The 1972 merger of the museums brought it important works that originally resided at the de Young, including a massive ebony cabinet by Pierre Gole (page 44) that remains one of the Museums' undeniable masterpieces, and a sofa made for Marie-Antoinette's *cabinet intérieur* at Versailles. The Legion shifted away from displaying sculpture and paintings separately, culminating in a 1995 reinstallation that traces the story of European art in an inclusive and linear fashion. The Porcelain Gallery, a favorite project of Spreckels's, has been enriched in recent decades by fine English and Continental works from Constance and Henry Bowles, for whom the gallery, recently refurbished, is now named (pages 80–81).

The decorative arts and sculpture collection continues to expand. With an agenda for acquiring only the finest objects, the Museums have procured fewer but more significant pieces in recent years, including a *secrétaire* (page 45) by the cabinetmaker Bernard II van Risamburgh, supplied to Lord Coventry on his visit to Paris in 1763.

Andrea della Robbia (Italian, 1437–1525)
Virgin and Child with Putti, ca. 1490–1495
Glazed terracotta relief
48 1/16 x 32 1/16 in. (122 x 81.5 cm)

Museum purchase, Alfred S. Wilsey Memorial Fund, 2003.1

Attributed to Benvenuto Cellini
(Italian, 1500–1571)
Portrait Bust of Cosimo I de' Medici, Grand Duke of Tuscany, ca. 1548–1553
Pentelic marble
37 3/4 x 28 1/4 x 15 1/2 in. (95.9 x 71.8 x 39.4 cm)

Roscoe and Margaret Oakes Collection, 75.2.16

Pierre Gole (French, ca. 1620–1684)
Cabinet on stand, ca. 1650
Ebony, inlay of various woods, tinted ivory, colored hardstones, and gilt-bronze figures
90 1/2 x 87 1/2 x 30 in. (229.9 x 222.3 x 76.2 cm)

Gift of William Randolph Hearst, 47.20.2a–b

Bernard II van Risamburgh
(known as B.V.R.B.) (French, active
1696–1766)
Secrétaire à abattant (fall-front
writing desk), 1763
Wood, gilt bronze, silvered bronze,
steel, marble, and silk
51 9/16 x 40 15/16 x 17 5/16 in.
(131 x 104 x 44 cm)

Museum purchase, European Art Trust
Fund and gift of Mrs. Margaret G.
Hindes Molarsky in memory of Barrett
G. Hindes, by exchange, 2010.35

Déjeuner chinois réticulé (tea and coffee service)
French, Sèvres Porcelain Factory, marks for 1839 and 1842
Hard-paste porcelain, enamel, gilding, and platinum
Serving tray: 6 1/2 x 19 3/4 x 19 3/4 in. (16.5 x 50.2 x 50.2 cm)

European Art Trust Fund, K. Hart Smith Bequest, Ruth L. and Alfred B. Koch Trust, Hildegard Seidel Bequest, European Decorative Arts Council, San Francisco Ceramic Circle, various tribute funds, Mrs. Clarence Sterling Postley, funds in memory of Nini Tobin Martin, Loretta Beckman-Carr Bequest, and Fine Arts Museums Foundation Auction Proceeds, 2009.11.1–10

Auguste Rodin (French, 1840–1917)
The Thinker, 1904
Cast bronze
72 x 38 x 54 in. (182.9 x
96.5 x 137.2 cm)

Gift of Alma de Bretteville Spreckels,
1924.18.1

FRENCH PERIOD ROOMS

THE LEGION GALLERIES hold three permanent installations of French interiors: a small Louis XIV cabinet made up of painted panels, dating from about 1680; the Rouen Room shown here, composed of paneling in the Rococo style, from about 1750; and a spectacular salon, a neoclassical masterpiece dating from about 1781, originally from the Hôtel de la Trémoille, Paris. The museum has lately been conducting extensive research on the original interior architecture and furnishings of these rooms to reconsider and present them to visitors with the greatest possible historical accuracy and aesthetic splendor, according to the individual character and qualities of each.

THE SKINNER ORGAN

SOLO 4
SOLO 16
TREMOLO
SOLO UNISON OFF
CLARION 4
VOX HUMANA 8
TUBA MAJOR 8
ENGLISH HORN 8
MILITARY TRUMPET 8
TUBA PROFUNDA 16
FRENCH HORN 8

THE PIPE ORGAN in the Rodin Gallery was designed and built by the Ernest M. Skinner Organ Company in Boston. One of the few indoor/outdoor organs ever built, it brings to life a wide repertoire of music, both in the galleries and the courtyard, during free concerts presented to museum visitors on weekends and occasionally on holidays.

John D. Spreckels commissioned the organ to honor his brother Adolph B. Spreckels and the museum that he and his wife were giving to the city. On the side of the organ console is a bronze dedication plaque by the artist Melvin Earl Cummings; it reads, "John D. Spreckels has generously given the organ in this temple for the pleasure of those who, like himself, are lovers of music. AD MCMXXIV." The organ was presented to the people of San Francisco in 1924; unfortunately, Adolph Spreckels died before either it or the museum could be completed. At that time organ concerts were extremely popular, and free access to such music in a museum on the West Coast was highly unusual. The presence of an instrument of this quality at the Legion added to its reputation as a "temple" of culture.

Ernest Skinner worked with the museum's architect, George Applegarth, to plan for the accommodation of the more than 4,500 organ pipes within the building. Ranging in size from half an inch to thirty-two feet (see pages 54–55), the pipes are concealed behind a canvas apse painted to look like marble, through which sound carries into the rotunda. The plaster frieze over the main entrance to the museum can be opened to allow the music to enter the Court of Honor as well. With its beautiful console made of walnut and mahogany and its ivory and ebony keys and stops, the organ represents the pinnacle of the Skinner Organ Company's output.

Like the museum building itself, the organ was damaged during the 1989 Loma Prieta earthquake. Magnificently restored under the direction of Edward Millington Stout with the ongoing support of the Lynde and Harry Bradley Foundation, this "king of instruments" continues to regularly fill the Legion of Honor with its orchestral-quality sound.

PEDAL
OCTAVE

EUROPEAN ART GALLERIES

THE INTERIOR ARCHITECTURE of the Legion of Honor creates some of the most beautiful museum spaces anywhere. Based on the aesthetic of the exterior's Beaux-Arts design, the grand proportions, coved ceilings, and elegant detailing of the Legion galleries provide the perfect setting for the traditional arts of Europe.

The architectural elements in this succession of interconnected spaces, called an enfilade, establish a classical symmetry that imposes a quiet

dignity on the installation. Capitalizing on the repetition of geometric shapes, designers and curators play with color variations and the placement of "vista pieces" to entice visitors to explore the sweep of galleries.

Here museumgoers encounter a progression of works ranging from the medieval to the modern. Paintings, sculptures, and decorative arts are all installed together to present an integrated view of each period's artistic output.

THE SPANISH CEILING

ORIGINALLY FROM ONE of the towers of the Palacio de Altamira in Torrijos, near Toledo, Spain, this magnificent ceiling was given to the Fine Arts Museums by the heirs of Charles Deering in 1946. Deering had purchased it from the ruins of the Palacio in 1906 and installed it in his home in Sitges, near Barcelona. When he returned to the United States in 1921 he had the ceiling packed up and sent to Chicago; it remained there until his heirs gave it to the de Young, where it was installed in 1948 and remained until 1989.

The ceiling underwent extensive restoration before it was reinstalled in the renovated Legion of Honor in 1995. Intensive cleaning, structural integration, and partial regilding, as well as reproduction of missing sections, brought the ceiling to its present splendor. A companion ceiling from another of the Spanish palace's four towers is at the Victoria and Albert Museum in London.

The ceiling, dating between 1482 and 1503, was built in the Hispano-Moresque style, a blend of Christian and Islamic architecture. The elaborate geometric pattern is Islamic in origin, but Christian motifs are also evident. The dome, eighteen feet in diameter, weighs about four thousand pounds, and the height of each of its eight triangular segments is approximately ten feet. At the center of each of the four wall panels is a coat of arms of the Maqueda family, members of the court of Isabella the Catholic. One pair shows the arms of Don Gutierre and the other, those of his wife, Doña Teresa, who was extremely devout. The gilt scallop shells around the top of the wall panels may refer to her piety; shells were particularly associated with pilgrimages to the shrine of Saint James at Santiago de Compostela, as they were used by pilgrims for eating and drinking and as alms plates.

European Painting

The Legion of Honor houses one of the great collections of European art in the United States. Approximately two hundred fifty of the Museums' more than seven hundred European paintings are on display in the beautiful Beaux-Arts building alongside their contemporary sculpture and decorative arts, offering a comprehensive survey of European artistic accomplishment from antiquity to the early twentieth century and encompassing world-class examples by many leading masters.

The holdings of European paintings were consolidated from collections built independently at the de Young and the Legion before the museums' merger. Many of the de Young's works, including William-Adolphe Bouguereau's *The Broken Pitcher* and Konstantin Makovsky's *The Russian Bride's Attire* (page 67), derived from the 1894 California Midwinter International Exposition and subsequent gifts by the museum's founder, Michael H. de Young. This selection was enriched over the years by gifts from the Samuel H. Kress Foundation, including works by El Greco, Tiziano Vecellio (Titian), Giovanni Battista Tiepolo, and Francisco de Goya, as well as paintings given by Roscoe and Margaret Oakes, who not only presented the museum with several masterworks but also established an acquisition endowment that continues to fund collection growth today.

The Legion had a European—and more specifically French—bias from the start due to the interests of its benefactor, Alma de Bretteville Spreckels. She provided paintings from her own holdings and enlisted donations from friends such as Mildred Anna and Henry K. S. Williams. Mr. and Mrs. Williams bequeathed their collection to the museum and created its first substantial acquisition fund, enabling later purchases of works by Pierre-Auguste Renoir, Édouard Manet, Jean-Antoine Watteau, Paul Cézanne, and others. Subsequent major gifts by collectors such as Mr. and Mrs. Prentis Cobb Hale, Dr. T. Edward and Tullah Hanley, and William H. Noble further elevated the status of the museum's holdings in European paintings.

After the museums merged, their European collections were united and showcased in the Legion's elegantly proportioned galleries. There unfolds a rich, sweeping visual chronology of European art in all its forms. Highlights of the paintings collection include a superb group of Dutch and Flemish seventeenth-century pictures, such as the Rembrandt van Rijn portrait *Joris de Caulerij* (page 66); many fine examples of French eighteenth-century painting by Watteau, Jean-Honoré Fragonard, Jean-Marc Nattier (page 62), Elisabeth Louise Vigée-LeBrun, and others; model works from the Golden Age of English portraiture by Sir Joshua Reynolds and Thomas Gainsborough; and notable British paintings from the Victorian era, such as John Roddam Spencer Stanhope's *Love and the Maiden* and John Fitzgerald's *Fairies in a Bird's Nest*.

The Legion is also home to a number of masterpieces from the nineteenth century. While some adhere to traditional conventions, paintings by Manet, Jean-Baptiste-Camille Corot, Honoré Daumier, and Edgar Degas reveal early glimmers of the social realism, fluid brushwork, and decorative abstraction embraced by Impressionism and Post-Impressionism. Georges Seurat's *Eiffel Tower* (page 68), Claude Monet's *Water Lilies* (page 69), and other key works epitomize these movements and set the stage for the artistic revolutions of the twentieth century, showcased by modern achievements such as Pablo Picasso's *Still Life with Skull, Leeks, and Pitcher*.

Lorenzo di Niccolò (possibly the Master of the Lazzaroni Madonna)
(Florentine, active 1392–1411)
Childbirth tray (*desco da parto*) with Diana and Actaeon (recto) and Justice (verso), ca. 1380–1400
Tempera and gold leaf on panel
25 1/8 x 25 3/8 in. (63.8 x 64.5 cm)

Gift of the Roscoe and Margaret Oakes Foundation, 78.78

Left: Rembrandt van Rijn (Dutch, 1606–1669)
Joris de Caulerij, 1632
Oil on canvas transferred to panel
40 1/2 x 33 3/16 in. (102.9 x 84.3 cm)

Roscoe and Margaret Oakes Collection, 66.31

Konstantin Makovsky (Russian, 1839–1915)
The Russian Bride's Attire, 1889
Oil on canvas
110 x 147 in. (279.4 x 373.4 cm)

Bequest of M. H. de Young, 53161

Georges Seurat (French, 1859–1891)
Eiffel Tower, ca. 1889
Oil on panel
9 1/2 x 6 in. (24.1 x 15.2 cm)

Museum purchase, William H. Noble Bequest Fund, 1979.48

Claude Monet (French, 1840–1926)
Water Lilies, ca. 1914–1917
Oil on canvas
65 3/8 x 56 in. (166.1 x 142.2 cm)

Museum purchase, Mildred Anna Williams Collection, 1973.3

ROSEKRANS COURT

MANY TEMPORARY EXHIBITIONS begin dramatically in Rosekrans Court before continuing into the surrounding galleries. Rosekrans Court is named for Mr. and Mrs. John N. Rosekrans Jr. Grandson of the Legion of Honor's founders, John joined his wife, Dodie, in chairing the campaign to raise the private funds needed to support the enormous project of the museum's 1995 renovation.

The skylight formed by the pyramid in the courtyard above brings controlled natural illumination to this part of the lower floor, including the adjacent galleries. Screens can reduce the brightness to prevent damage to works of art that are light sensitive. Though it is rarely fully uncovered, the skylight brings an openness to the space that belies its underground location.

PARIS

Ancient Art

ANCIENT ART at the Fine Arts Museums of San Francisco is showcased on the Legion's lower level and covers a broad geographical and chronological spectrum within the ancient Mediterranean world, with a special focus on Egypt, the Near East, Greece, the Aegean Islands, Rome, and Etruria. It encompasses a diverse array of art forms—including sculptures, figurines, vessels, jewelry, and reliefs—crafted in an equally varied range of materials, from stone, metal, and ivory to terracotta, wood, and glass.

Though these works are now housed exclusively at the Legion of Honor, both Michael H. de Young, founder of the de Young, and Alma de Bretteville Spreckels, founder of the Legion, furnished the collections with rare and beautiful antiquities, considered essential to any art museum in the late nineteenth and early twentieth centuries. De Young retained a number of ancient works from the California Midwinter International Exposition, or purchased them with its profits—including a rare granodiorite torso of a god (1363–1353 BC) (page 75) made during the reign of Egypt's "Dazzling Sun," Amenhotep III, and at the zenith of New Kingdom art. Among the first and largest gifts of ancient art given to the Legion was a group of primarily classical antiquities, which Spreckels received from her friend Elisabeth, the queen of Greece. The early formation of the collection's core rewarded the Museums with many important pieces that would be difficult to acquire today.

Subsequent museum directors and curators have nonetheless built remarkably on the founders' initial efforts. Although the collection of antiquities is relatively small, it provides an excellent introduction to the art of the cultures represented and establishes a firm basis for appreciating the forms and iconography that shaped Western art. A number of the department's holdings are considered among the finest of their type, such as the carved stone "winged genius" from the walls of the lavishly decorated Northwest Palace of Ashurnasirpal II (ca. 879 BC) (pages 76–77), and the rare, exquisitely carved ivory plaques from the Palace of Shalmaneser III (8th–7th century BC) (page 77), both located in the Assyrian capital city of Nimrud. Over the past three decades the collection has grown to encompass many more scarce and beautiful objects from the ancient Mediterranean world.

Additional highlights from the collection include an exquisitely carved and inscribed Egyptian cedar anthropoid coffin from Dynasty 30 (380–343 BC) (page 78), a Persian relief of a gift bearer from the fabled Achaemenid capital city of Persepolis (490–470 BC) (page 72), a virtuoso fourth-century red-figure volute krater (page 78) skillfully painted with a scene from Homer's *Iliad* by one of the most important Greek vase painters in South Italy, and a dramatically draped statue of Asklepios, god of medicine, showing the increased realism characteristic of sculpture from the Hellenistic period (page 79).

Cycladic figure, ca. 2500 BC
Greek, Cyclades, Keros culture, attributed to the Goulandris Master
Marble
H. 13⅜ in. (34 cm)

Museum purchase, William H. Noble Bequest Fund, 1981.42

Torso of a god, 1363–1353 BC
Egyptian
Granodiorite
38 x 18¼ x 13¼ in. (96.5 x 46.4 x 33.7 cm)

Museum purchase, M. H. de Young Endowment Fund, 54661

Above: Nimrud ivory plaque with winged human-headed sphinx, 8th–7th century BC
Syro-Phoenician, Fort Shalmaneser, Nimrud
Ivory
4 3/16 x 1 3/4 in. (10.7 x 4.4 cm)

From the British School of Archaeology in Iraq. Museum purchase, William H. Noble Bequest Fund, 1980.54.1

Left: "Winged genius" from the Northwest Palace of Ashurnasirpal II, ca. 879 BC
Assyrian, Nimrud
Bituminous limestone
30 x 41 1/8 in. (76.2 x 104.5 cm)

Museum purchase, Roscoe and Margaret Oakes Income Fund and the Walter H. and Phyllis J. Shorenstein Foundation Fund, 1995.47

Left: Anthropoid coffin, Dynasty 30, 380–343 BC
Egyptian
Cedar with traces of paint
78 x 24 x 19½ in. (198.1 x 61 x 49.5 cm)

Museum purchase, gift of Diane B. Wilsey in memory of Alfred S. Wilsey, 2002.2a–b

Above: Red-figure volute krater (wine vessel), ca. 330–320 BC
Greek, South Italy, Apulia, attributed to the Baltimore Painter
Terracotta
42⅝ x 23 x 17¾ in. (108.3 x 58.4 x 45.1 cm)

Museum purchase, Dorothy Spreckels Munn Fund, 2005.24a–b

Greek, Hellenistic period
Pentelic marble
36 x 14 1/2 x 9 in. (91.4 x 36.8 x 22.9 cm)

Museum purchase, United Hellenic American Congress and the William H. Noble Bequest Fund, 1981.41

CONSTANCE AND HENRY BOWLES
PORCELAIN GALLERY
BASKETS FOR DESSERT SERVICE
1 Pierced basket with turquoise interior
NEW ACQUISITION
2 Pair of baskets, royal blue interior
3 Tea bowl and saucer, red hop trellis
4 Two-handled cup and saucer

PORCELAIN HAS BEEN a part of the Legion's collections since founder Alma de Bretteville Spreckels first began gathering objects for her museum. Consistent with her great interest in the arts of France, Spreckels's earliest focus in this area was on the productions of the Sèvres manufactory. Subsequent gifts to the collection included porcelain and pottery from England and continental Europe, some dating from the Renaissance, but with an emphasis on the eighteenth century.

The Bowles Porcelain Gallery, named to honor the gift of the Constance and Henry Bowles Collection, reopened in 2009 after an extensive renovation and reinstallation. The first section of the gallery is dedicated to English porcelain, from the early days of the Chelsea factory to the still-active Worcester factory. The back of the gallery displays Continental porcelain and pottery, including the Bowles collection of Chantilly, as well as examples of Meissen, Sèvres, and majolica from Renaissance Italy.

Although this room is housed on the museum's lower level, it is flooded with natural light, and many visitors consider it the most beautiful spot in the building. Adjoining the gallery is the Porcelain Study Room, which houses examples of English, French, and German pottery and porcelain, as well as Chinese export wares, all displayed in glass-fronted wall cabinets. This room is available for study by appointment.

THE REVA AND DAVID LOGAN
GALLERY OF ILLUSTRATED BOOKS

THIS SMALL GALLERY on the Legion's lower level honors the collection of artists' books assembled by Reva and David Logan and given to the Museums for the education and enjoyment of the public, under the curatorial and conservation care of the Achenbach Foundation for Graphic Arts.

A regular rotation of books from the Logan Collection, as well as selective loans, reveals the rich variety found in this special art form. Many of the installations in this gallery further illuminate the themes explored in the museum's larger special exhibitions.

The Achenbach Foundation for Graphic Arts

THE ACHENBACH FOUNDATION for Graphic Arts is widely recognized as one of the most notable collections of prints, drawings, and artists' books in the United States. The department's strength derives from its diversity—with nearly one hundred thousand objects representing over five hundred years of graphic arts from around the world, the Achenbach's broad range of works on paper reflects the aesthetics, politics, and social and cultural mores of a wide variety of eras and geographical locations.

The Achenbach Foundation is named for Moore and Hazel Achenbach, who gave the bulk of their collection to the city of San Francisco in 1948 and the remainder upon Mr. Achenbach's death in 1963. The Achenbachs intended to systematically illustrate the entire development of the graphic arts from the fifteenth century to the present day, and curators of the department have worked steadily over the years to realize this goal, filling gaps and moving the collection into the twenty-first century through gifts, purchases, and the generous support of additional donors. Today the Achenbach is the largest repository of works of art on paper in the western United States. Highlights include special collections of Japanese prints and Russian theater and dance materials, as well as sizable holdings of modern and contemporary prints and books.

The Achenbach also houses significant archives and collections such as the Crown Point Press Archive, which includes one impression from every print edition published by the press, as well as many additional works; the Anderson collection of American graphic arts from the mid-twentieth century onward, developed by Harry W. and Mary Margaret Anderson and their daughter, Mary Patricia Anderson Pence; the Ed Ruscha Graphic Arts Archive; and the Reva and David Logan Collection of modern artists' books.

In the areas of drawings, watercolors, pastels, and other unique works on paper, the department is particularly strong in

American and European examples from the nineteenth and twentieth centuries. A gift from Dr. T. Edward and Tullah Hanley, presented in 1969, includes important sheets by Paul Gauguin, Edgar Degas, and Henri de Toulouse-Lautrec; and gifts from Mr. and Mrs. John D. Rockefeller 3rd in 1979 and 1993 enriched the collection with watercolors by major American artists such as Winslow Homer, Charles Burchfield, and Andrew Wyeth.

The de Young and the Legion of Honor present selections from this collection in rotating exhibitions and installations housed in specially designated galleries. Works not on view are stored along with the photography holdings in the Achenbach's state-of-the-art facilities at the Legion. The collection's depth and breadth have made it an important resource for the Museums, which frequently draw upon it to enrich and contextualize their special exhibitions.

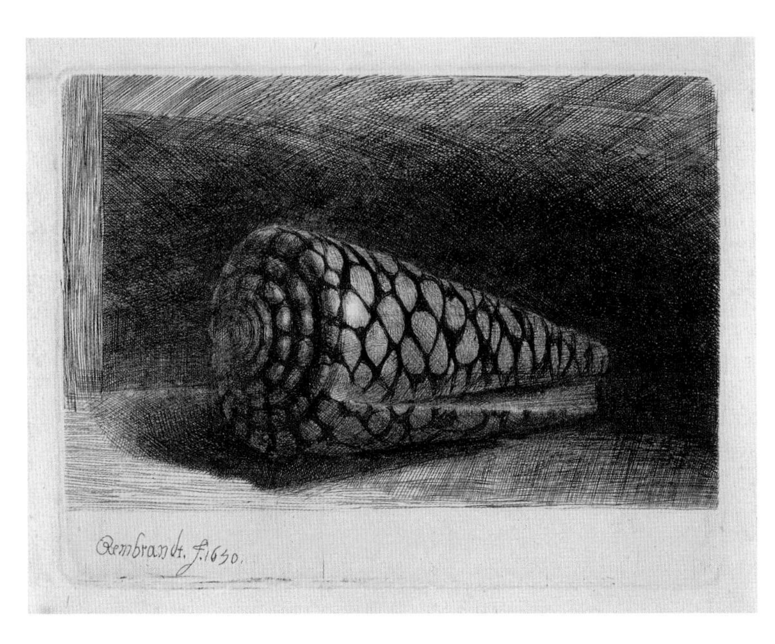

Rembrandt van Rijn (Dutch, 1606–1669)
The Shell (Conus marmoreus), 1650
Etching, drypoint, and engraving
Sheet: 4 7/16 x 5 3/4 in. (11.3 x 14.6 cm)

Museum purchase, gift of Dr. T. Edward and Tullah Hanley by exchange, Achenbach Foundation for Graphic Arts Endowment Fund, and anonymous bequest, 1997.42

Hyacinthe Rigaud (French, 1659–1743)
Sheet of Studies of Hands Playing Bagpipes and Drapery, 1735
Black chalk with white chalk on blue laid paper
Sheet: 11¾ x 17¾ in. (29.8 x 45.1 cm)

Gift of Mr. and Mrs. Sidney M. Ehrman, 1953.34

Winslow Homer (American, 1836–1910)
Burnt Mountain, 1892
Watercolor with traces of graphite on paper
13 15/16 x 20 in. (35.4 x 50.8 cm)

Gift of Mr. and Mrs. John D. Rockefeller 3rd, 1979.7.55

Fernand Léger (French, 1881–1955)
Illustration in the book *La fin du monde, filmée par l'ange N.D.*, by Blaise Cendrars (Paris: Editions de la Sirène, 1919), 1919
Color pochoir and line-block reproduction on paper
Sheet: 12 5/8 x 9 13/16 in. (32 x 25 cm)

Gift of the Reva and David Logan Foundation, 1998.40.77.10

Ed Ruscha (American, b. 1937)
Trial proof for *Standard Station*, 1966
Color screenprint on paper
25 5/8 x 40 in. (65.1 x 101.6 cm)

Museum purchase, Mrs. Paul L. Wattis Fund, 2000.131.5.1

Richard Diebenkorn (American, 1922–1993)
Green, 1986
Color aquatint, spit-bite aquatint, soap-ground aquatint, and drypoint on Somerset paper
Printed by Marcia Bartholme
Published by Crown Point Press
Sheet: 53 11/16 x 40 3/4 in. (136.4 x 103.5 cm)

Crown Point Press Archive, gift of Crown Point Press, 1991.28.1274

FLORENCE GOULD THEATER

The architect for the Legion of Honor, George Applegarth, designed this circular, jewel-box theater on the lower floor of the museum and decorated it in the style of Louis XVI. The memorial theme of the building is echoed in the ceiling mural, *The Apotheosis of the California Soldier,* by Spanish artist Julio Vila y Prades, who was once a student of the famous Joaquín Sorolla y Bastida.

Florence Gould was a friend of Alma de Bretteville Spreckels, who had hoped Mrs. Gould would one day offer her important collection of art to the museum. Mrs. Gould's will, however, stipulated that the collection be sold to fund her foundation. After the deaths of both patrons, Spreckels's grandson John Rosekrans learned that her foundation could supply grants to institutions that furthered French culture; he succeeded in bringing some of the Gould fortune to the museum after all. The original "Little Theater" underwent a major restoration supervised by another Spreckels grandson, architect Adolph Rosekrans, and funded largely by the Florence Gould Foundation. It was rededicated as the Florence Gould Theater in 1987.

The three-hundred-seat theater was further restored with excellent acoustics during the renovation of the entire museum in 1995. Today it continues to offer an intimate setting for lectures, plays, and musical performances.

LEGION OF HONOR MUSEUM STORE

The Museum Store across from the café features a broad selection of art books, posters, stationery, jewelry, and other gift items related to the museum's collections and exhibitions. Additional stores often accompany temporary exhibitions and offer related books and gift items that complement the museum's educational mission by further illuminating the artworks on display.

Duck! Rabbit!
MY MONSTER NOTEBOOK
GREECE! ROME! MONSTERS!
PIRANESI

SOURCES AND FURTHER READING

De Caso, Jacques, and Patricia B. Sanders. *Rodin's Sculpture: A Critical Study of the Spreckels Collection. California Palace of the Legion of Honor.* San Francisco: Fine Arts Museums of San Francisco and Charles E. Tuttle, Rutland, VT, 1977.

Dreyfus, Renée. *California Palace of the Legion of Honor.* San Francisco: Fine Arts Museums of San Francisco, 1995.

——. *Legion of Honor: Selected Works.* San Francisco: Fine Arts Museums of San Francisco in association with Scala, London, 2007.

Fine Arts Museums of San Francisco: Selected Works. San Francisco: Fine Arts Museums of San Francisco, 1987.

Johnson, Robert Flynn, Karin Breuer, and Joseph R. Goldyne. *Treasures of the Achenbach Foundation for Graphic Arts.* San Francisco: Fine Arts Museums of San Francisco, 1995.

Johnson, Robert Flynn, and Donna Stein. *Artists' Books in the Modern Era 1870–2000: The Reva and David Logan Collection of Illustrated Books.* San Francisco: Fine Arts Museums of San Francisco in association with Thames & Hudson, London, 2001.

Nash, Steven A., Lynn Federle Orr, and Marion C. Stewart. *Masterworks of European Painting in the California Palace of the Legion of Honor.* San Francisco: Fine Arts Museums of San Francisco in association with Hudson Hills Press, New York, 1999.

Rosenberg, Pierre, and Marion C. Stewart, with Thierry Lefrançois. *French Paintings 1500–1825. The Fine Arts Museums of San Francisco.* San Francisco: Fine Arts Museums of San Francisco, 1987.

Scharlach, Bernice. *Big Alma: San Francisco's Alma Spreckels.* San Francisco: Scottwall Associates, 1990.

Sutton, Denys, ed. *The Fine Arts Museums of San Francisco.* Originally published in *Apollo Magazine* 11, no. 216 (February 1980) and no. 217 (March 1980). Two issues bound as one publication.

ACKNOWLEDGMENTS

The Fine Arts Museums of San Francisco wish to thank the many individuals whose leadership and cooperation helped to make this book a reality, including Diane B. Wilsey, President of the Board of Trustees, as well as the officers at the Museums, Richard Benefield, Deputy Director; Michele Gutierrez-Canepa, Chief Administrative Officer and Chief Financial Officer; and Julian Cox, Founding Curator of Photography and Chief Administrative Curator.

The Museums also give thanks to our partners at Glue + Paper Workshop, Amanda Freymann and Joan Sommers, as well as our author, Ann Heath Karlstrom, and our proofreader, Susan Richmond. At the Museums, Danica Hodge managed the production, with extensive assistance from Lucy Medrich. We also thank Karen Levine, former Director of Publications, who began this project, and Leslie Dutcher, Director of Publications, who completed it.

The Museums' curatorial staff made essential contributions to sections pertaining to their respective departments, including Lynn Federle Orr and Melissa Buron for European painting; Martin Chapman and Maria Santangelo for European decorative arts and sculpture; Renée Dreyfus and Louise Chu for ancient art; and Karin Breuer, James Ganz, and Colleen Terry for works on paper.

Additional staff who aided in this project include Stuart Hata and Tim Niedert, from the Museum Stores, who made excellent suggestions during the conceptual and production phases of the book; Patty Lacson, Greg Zaharoff, Mike Badger and the Museums' engineering staff, and Hugo Gray and the Museums' security staff, who all provided support during new photography of the building; and Sue Grinols, Joe McDonald, Jorge Bachmann, Debra Evans, Jane Glover, and Andrew Fox, who all contributed additional photography.

Our esteemed photographer, Henrik Kam, and his colleagues provided impeccable services with patience and flexibility. Jim Jackson and James McCormick of San Francisco Recreation and Parks were gracious in aiding our building photography in Golden Gate Park; Helen Taylor, from the California Academy of Sciences, was helpful in arranging for us to shoot from that building's roof; and Thomas Sotelo and Rosalia Schoemaker from McCalls provided services on behalf of the Museum Cafés.

Finally, we would like to acknowledge many other individuals for their participation in this project: Neda Asgharzadeh, Liz Austerman, Renee Baldocchi, Brandon Ballog, Hannah Battat, Ashley Bedell, Victoria Binder, Rose Burke, Isabella Castillo, Louis Chan, Kelly Anne Chin, Bill Chow, Helen Chun, Morrison Chun, Stephen Chun, Rebecca Crump, Julia Doherty, William Doherty, Robert Gardali, Mark Garrett, Tasman Grant, Clara Hatcher, Ava Hodge, Emma Hosking, Sophia Hosking, Kathy Lassen-Hahne, Christopher Lentz, Susan Leurey, Jessica Lo, Jack Louie, Martin Luk, Peter Narodny, Zeynep Oguz, Zhen Liang Peng, Juliana Pennington, Sam Rogerson, Kristen Seki, Emmy Sharp, Gregory Stock, Travis White, Michael Wong, and Joseph Yan.

Page 8

Page 8: Auguste Rodin (French, 1840–1917). *The Age of Bronze*, ca. 1875–1877. Bronze, 71½ x 21¼ x 25½ in. (181.6 x 54 x 64.8 cm). Gift of Alma de Bretteville Spreckels, 1940.141

Page 26: Anna Hyatt Huntington (American, 1876–1973). *El Cid Campeador (Ruy Díaz de Bivar, 1040–1099)*, 1921. Bronze on granite base, 176¾ x 74 x 139⅜ in. (448.9 x 188 x 354 cm). Gift of Herbert Fleishhacker, 1937.11

Page 27: Anna Hyatt Huntington (American, 1876–1973). *Joan of Arc (Jeanne d'Arc)*, 1915. Bronze on granite base, 144⅛ x 45⅝ x 108⅞ in. (366.1 x 115.9 x 276.5 cm). Gift of Archer M. Huntington, 1926.160.

Page 31: Reproduction of *Laocoön* group (detail). European, early 20th century. Marble, 92 x 62 x 32 in. (233.7 x 157.5 x 81.3 cm). Bequest of James D. Phelan, 1931.40

Pages 34–35: Mark di Suvero (American, b. 1933). *Pax Jerusalemme*, 1998–1999. Painted steel, 300 x 540 x 240 in. (762 x 1371.6 x 609.6 cm). Museum purchase, Roscoe and Margaret Oakes Income Fund, 2000.43

Page 39: Auguste Rodin (French, 1840–1917). *The Three Shades* (detail), ca. 1898. Cast bronze, 75½ x 73½ x 41½ in. (191.8 x 186.7 x 105.4 cm). Collection of the City and County of San Francisco, gift of the Raphael Weill Memorial Committee, L95.74

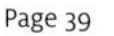

Page 39

Page 40: Peter Carl Fabergé (Russian, 1846–1920). Tea service and table (detail), ca. 1900. Silver gilt, Karelian birch, and ivory. Gift of Victoria Melita, Grand Duchess Kirill, through Alma de Bretteville Spreckels, 1945.355–366.1

Pages 50–51, 53: Ernest M. Skinner Organ Company (American). Pipe organ console (details), 1924. Walnut, mahogany, ivory, and ebony, 64¾ x 98 x 67½ in. (164.5 x 248.9 x 171.5 cm). Gift of John D. Spreckels, 1992.153

Page 40

Pages 56–57: (Left) Elisabeth Louise Vigée Le Brun (French, 1755–1842). *Hyacinthe Gabrielle Roland, Marchioness Wellesley (formerly Countess of Mornington)*, 1791. Oil on canvas. 39 x 29½ in. (99.1 x 74.9 cm). Museum purchase, Mildred Anna Williams Collection and Bequest Fund of Henry S. Williams in memory of H. K. S. Williams, 1991.29. (Center right) Francois Joseph Bosio (French, 1769–1845). *Portrait Bust of Le Marquis D'Aligre*, early 19th century. Bronze with marble base, 27½ x 19 x 12 in. (69.9 x 48.3 x 30.5 cm). Gift of Pierre David-Weill, 54.59a–b. (Far right) Francisco José de Goya y Lucientes (Spanish, 1746–1828). *Don Ramon de Posada y Soto*, ca. 1801. Oil on canvas, 43⅜ x 33¾ in. (110.2 x 85.7 cm). Gift of the Samuel H. Kress Foundation, 61.44.26

Pages 58–59, 61: Anonymous maker (Spanish, 1482–1503). Ceiling from the Palacio de Altamira. Painted, gilded, and composed wood, 225 x 225 in. (571.5 x 571.5 cm). Gift of Mrs. Richard Ely Danielson and Mrs. Chauncey McCormick, 46.16

Page 62

Page 62: Jean-Marc Nattier (French, 1685–1766). *Terpsichore, Muse of Music and Dance* (detail), ca. 1739. Oil on canvas, 53½ x 49¼ in. (135.9 x 125.1 cm). Museum purchase, Mildred Anna Williams Collection, 1954.60

Page 72: Relief of a gift bearer, ca. 490–470 BC. Persian, Persepolis, Achaemenid. Limestone, 8⅛ x 7½ x 4 in. (20.6 x 19.1 x 10.2 cm). Museum purchase, gift of Lisa Sardegna, Albert P. Wagner Bequest Fund, William A. Stimson, Friends of Ian White Endowment Income Fund, Unrestricted Art Acquisition Endowment Fund, Volunteer Council Acquisition Fund, Ancient Art Trust Fund and Auction Proceeds, Mrs. John N. Rosekrans Jr., Sande Schlumberger, Endowment Fund in Honor of Francesca and Thomas Carr Howe, Walter H. and Phyllis J. Shorenstein Foundation Fund, Tish and James Brown, and various tribute funds, 2008.1

Page 84

Page 84: Edgar Degas (French, 1834–1917). *Femme s'essuyant (Seated Bather Drying Her Neck)* (detail), ca. 1905–1910. Charcoal and pastel on tracing paper, 27 1/16 x 22⅞ in. (68.7 x 58.1 cm). Gift of Mrs. John Jay Ide, 1995.62

Published by the Fine Arts Museums of San Francisco

Fine Arts Museums of San Francisco
Golden Gate Park
50 Hagiwara Tea Garden Drive
San Francisco, CA 94118-4502
www.famsf.org

Leslie Dutcher, Director of Publications
Danica Hodge, Editor
Lucy Medrich, Associate Editor

Project Management by Danica Hodge
Copyedited by Lucy Medrich
Proofread by Susan Richmond

Produced by Glue + Paper Workshop LLC, Chicago
Designed and typeset by Joan Sommers
Production management by Amanda Freymann
Color separations by Professional Graphics, Inc.
Printed and bound in China by Asia Pacific Offset

Library of Congress Cataloging-in-Publication Data

Legion of Honor (San Francisco, Calif.)
Legion of Honor : inside and out / introduction by Ann Heath Karlstrom ; new photography by Henrik Kam.
pages cm
ISBN 978-0-88401-136-1
1. Legion of Honor (San Francisco, Calif.) I. Title.
N739.A835 2013
708.194'61—dc23
2012044807

Unless otherwise noted in the captions, all artworks reproduced in this book are from the collection of the Fine Arts Museums of San Francisco.

Dimensions for drawings and paintings indicate the size of the sheet or unframed canvas. Dimensions for prints and photographs document image size. Height precedes width. For three-dimensional objects, dimensions are listed in order of height, width, and depth.

Back cover, left to right: Nimrud ivory plaque with winged human-head sphinx, 8th–7th century BC, detail of page 77. The Legion's European art galleries, detail of a photograph by Steve Whittaker. Claude Monet, *Water Lilies*, ca. 1914–1917, detail of page 69

Photography Credits

New photography has been made possible by The Charles D. Field Endowment Fund. Frontispiece, title page, 24–25, 28–29, 30, 31, 32–33, 56–57, 92–93, 94–95, 96–97, 103: photographs by Henrik Kam, © FAMSF. Unless otherwise indicated, all other photographs are courtesy Imaging Department, © FAMSF. Copyright information pertaining to artworks is listed below.

Cover, 8, 36–37, 38: Steve Whittaker, © FAMSF. 6: Pamela J. Whitmer. 10: San Francisco History Center, San Francisco Public Library. 11, 13, 14, 16–17, 18, 19: FAMSF archives. 23, 58–59, 61: Richard Barnes/OTTO. 39: Drew Altizer. 47: Gregory Bertolini, courtesy Marketing and Communications Department. 50–51, 53: Andrew Fox, FAMSF. 89: © 2012 Artists Rights Society (ARS), New York/ADAGP, Paris. 90: © Ed Ruscha. 91: © The Richard Diebenkorn Foundation.